blur
PARKLIFE

GW00643758

1	**GIRLS & BOYS** PAGE 3	9	**TO THE END** PAGE 36
2	**TRACY JACKS** PAGE 10	10	**LONDON LOVES** PAGE 41
3	**END OF A CENTURY** PAGE 18	11	**TROUBLE IN THE MESSAGE CENTRE** PAGE 46
4	**PARKLIFE** PAGE 15	12	**CLOVER OVER DOVER** PAGE 51
5	**BANK HOLIDAY** PAGE 22	13	**MAGIC AMERICA** PAGE 56
6	**BADHEAD** PAGE 28	14	**JUBILEE** PAGE 61
7	**THE DEBT COLLECTOR** PAGE 26	15	**THIS IS A LOW** PAGE 66
8	**FAR OUT** PAGE 33	16	**LOT 105** PAGE 70

Wise Publications
London / New York / Paris / Sydney / Copenhagen / Madrid

Exclusive Distributors:
MUSIC SALES LIMITED 8/9 Frith Street, London W1V 5TZ, England. MUSIC SALES PTY. LIMITED 120 Rothschild Avenue, Rosebery, NSW 2018, Australia.

Order No. AM92132 ISBN 0-7119-4276-5
Book designed by MICHAEL BELL DESIGN. Original album designed by STYLOROUGE. Music arranged by ROGER DAY. Music processed by PAUL EWERS MUSIC DESIGN.
Front cover photography by BOB THOMAS SPORTS. Back cover photography by PAUL POSTLE.

Your Guarantee of Quality:
As publishers, we strive to produce every book to the highest commercial standards.
The music has been freshly engraved and, whilst endeavouring to retain the original running order of the album, this book has been carefully designed to minimise awkward page turns
and to make playing from it a real pleasure. Particular care has been given to specifying acid-free, neutral-sized paper made from pulps which have not been elemental chlorine bleached.
This pulp is from farmed sustainable forests and was produced with special regard for the environment. Throughout, the printing and binding have been planned to ensure a sturdy,
attractive publication which should give years of enjoyment. If your copy fails to meet our high standards, please inform us and we will gladly replace it.

Music Sales' complete catalogue describes thousands of titles and is available in full colour sections by subject, direct from Music Sales Limited.
Please state your areas of interest and send a cheque/postal order for £1.50 for postage to: MUSIC SALES LIMITED, Newmarket Road, Bury St. Edmunds, Suffolk IP33 3YB.
Printed in the United Kingdom by J.B. Offset Printers (Marks Tey) Limited, Marks Tey, Essex.

1 GIRLS & BOYS

Words & Music by Damon Albarn, Graham Coxon, Alex James & David Rowntree

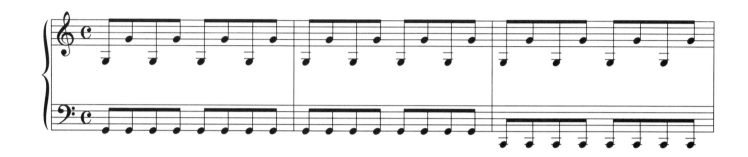

1. Streets like a jun - gle,
(Verse 2 see block lyric)

so call the po - lice,—

fol - low - ing the herd

down to Greece,-

on ho - li - day. Love in the nine - ties,

Verse 2:
Avoiding all work
Because there's none available.
Like battery thinkers
Count their thoughts on 1 2 3 4 5 fingers.
Nothing is wasted,
Only reproduced,
You get nasty blisters
Du bist sehr schön,
But we haven't been introduced.

2 | TRACY JACKS

Words & Music by Damon Albarn, Graham Coxon, Alex James & David Rowntree

1. Tra - cy Jacks works in Ci - vil Ser - vice, Tra - cy Jacks, it's
(Verses 2 & 3 see block lyric)

Verse 2:

Tracy Jacks
Left home without warning,
Tracy Jacks
At five in the morning
Tracy Jacks
Got on the first train to Walton
Tracy Jacks
And stood on the sea front laughing.
Tracy Jacks
Threw his clothes in the water
Tracy Jacks
And ran around naked
Tracy Jacks
Was stopped by the police
Tracy Jacks
And escorted back home.

Verse 3:

Tracy Jacks
Ooh, ooh, ooh, ooh
Tracy Jacks
Ooh, ooh, ooh, ooh
Tracy Jacks
Ooh, ooh, ooh, ooh
Tracy Jacks
Ooh, ooh, ooh, ooh
Tracy Jacks
Ooh, ooh, ooh, ooh
Tracy Jacks
Ooh, ooh, ooh, ooh
Tracy Jacks
Ooh, ooh, ooh, ooh
Tracy Jacks
Ooh, ooh, ooh, ooh.

4 PARKLIFE

Words & Music by Damon Albarn, Graham Coxon, Alex James & David Rowntree

1. *(Spoken)* Confidence is a preference for the habitual voyeur of what is known as park - life.
(Verse 2 see block lyric)

And morning soup can be avoided if you take a route straight through what is known as park - life.

John's got brewer's droop, he gets intimidated by the dirty pigeons; they love a bit of it, park - life.

Who's that gut lord marching; you should cut down on your porklife mate, get some exercise.

CHORUS

All the peo - ple, so ma - ny peo - ple, they

all go hand in hand,— hand in hand through their park - life.

To Coda ⊕

D.%. al Coda ⊕ Coda
(repeat chorus)

2. play 4 times

(park - life)   (park - life)

(Spoken 3 & 4) { It's got nothing to do with your vorsprung durch technic, you know,
and it's not about you joggers who go round and round and round.

Verse 2:
I get up when I want except on Wednesday when I get rudely awakened by the dustmen - (park life)
I put my trousers on, have a cup of tea and I think about leaving the house. - (park life)
I feed the pigeons, I sometimes feed the sparrows too. It gives me a sense of enormous well-being - (park life)
And then I'm happy for the rest of the day safe in the knowledge there will always be a bit of my heart devoted to it.

3 END OF A CENTURY

Words & Music by Damon Albarn, Graham Coxon, Alex James & David Rowntree

good morn-ing T. V., ____ you're look-ing so health - y. ____

We all say, don't want to be ___ a - lone, ___ we wear the same clothes 'cause we feel ___ the same

and kiss with dry lips when we say ___ good - night, ___ end of a cen - tury

oh, _____ it's no-thing spe - cial.

Verse 2:
Sex on the T.V.
Everybody's at it,
And the mind gets dirty
As you get closer to thirty.
He gives her a cuddle,
They're glowing in a huddle,
Good night T.V. you're all made up
And you're looking like me.

5 BANK HOLIDAY

Words & Music by Damon Albarn, Graham Coxon, Alex James & David Rowntree

⊕ *Coda*

Bank ho - li - day.

Verse 2:
Barbecue is cooking
Sausages and chicken,
The patio is buzzing,
The neighbours they are looking,
John is down the fun pub
Drinking lots of lager,
Girls and boys are on the game,
All the high streets look the same.

7 THE DEBT COLLECTOR

Words & Music by Damon Albarn, Graham Coxon, Alex James & David Rowntree

Counter melody on 𝄋.only

D.%. thru' and repeat back to fade

6 | BADHEAD

Words & Music by Damon Albarn, Graham Coxon, Alex James & David Rowntree

1. So far I've not real-ly stayed in touch,
(Verse 2 see block lyric - 3° instrumental)

well you knew as much, it's no sur-prise

ar - gu - ment.— And in a - ny case I'd ra - ther wear— it, it's like a

bad head in the morn - ing.

Verse 2:
And you, you've not really stayed in touch,
Well I knew as much, it's no surprise
That today I'll get up around two
With nothing to do except get a touch of flu.

Verse 3: - instrumental

8 FAR OUT

Words & Music by Damon Albarn, Graham Coxon, Alex James & David Rowntree

Words & Music by Damon Albarn, Graham Coxon, Alex James & David Rowntree

All these dir - ty words, (Jusqu'à la

fin) they make us look so dumb (En plein sol -

eil) been drink - ing far too much (Jusqu'à la

fin) and nei - ther of us mean what we say. (En plein a -

Verse 2:
What happened to us *Jusqu'à la fin*
Soon it will be gone forever *En plein soleil*
Infatuated only with ourselves *Jusqu'à la fin*
And neither of us can think straight any more *En plein amour.*

10 LONDON LOVES

Words & Music by Damon Albarn, Graham Coxon, Alex James & David Rowntree

1. A me-lo-dy has ta-ken him ov-er,
(Verse 2 see block lyric)

cough-ing tar in his Ja-pan-ese mo-tor,

the lights are ma-gic and he feels luck-y,

and he's got mo-ney, cheats like an ar-row.

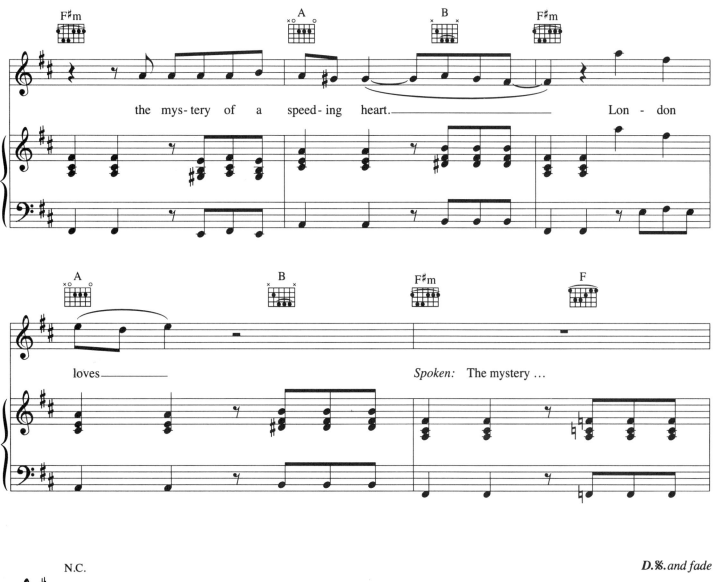

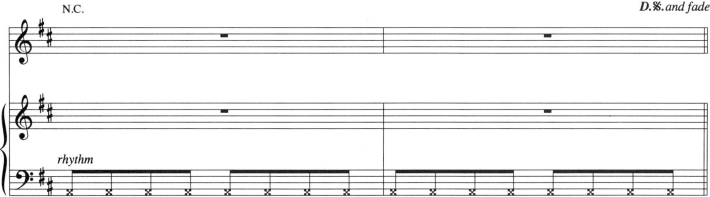

Verse 2:
It's love-u-like and everyone's at it,
And words are cheap when the mind is elastic
He loves the violence, keeps ticking over
So sleep together before today is sold for ever.

11 TROUBLE IN THE MESSAGE CENTRE

Words & Music by Damon Albarn, Graham Coxon, Alex James & David Rowntree

trou - ble._____ So much trou - ble. A new type face, a

new day___ in so much trou - - ble,_____

___ you can't re - mem - ber ten min - utes a - go,___ in so much

trou - - ble,_____ too much trou - ble. La la la la la___

play 4 times

tacet 1° & 2°

49

Verse 2:
I am a manager,
And I am in control
As the local delegator
(no calls today dear, they'll just have to wait dear)
I offer no guarantee at all
(so don't take it lightly, it must be sold one day).

Words & Music by Damon Albarn, Graham Coxon, Alex James & David Rowntree

1. I'm on the white cliffs of Do - ver,   think-ing it ov - er and ov -
(Verses 2 & 3 see block lyric)

- er,   and if I jump then it's ov - er,

Verse 2:
I'd like to roll in the clover
With you over and over
On the white cliffs of Dover
And then I'd let you push me over.

Verse 3:
And now the bluebirds are over
Over the white cliffs of Dover
And when you push me over
Don't bury me, I'm not worth anything.

13 MAGIC AMERICA

Words & Music by Damon Albarn, Graham Coxon, Alex James & David Rowntree

1. Bill Bar-ret has a sim-ple dream,— he calls it his— plan B.—
(Verses 2 & 3 see block lyric)

— Where there are build-ings in the sky— and the

air is su-gar free, and ev-'ry-one's ve-ry

Repeat to fade

Verse 2:
Well plan B arrived on a holiday
Took a cab to the shopping malls
Bought and ate till he could do neither any more
Then he found love on Channel 44.

Verse 3:
Bill Barret sent his postcards home
To everyone he's ever known,
They read "fifty nine cents gets you a good square meal
From the people who care how you feel."

14 JUBILEE

Words & Music by Damon Albarn, Graham Coxon, Alex James & David Rowntree

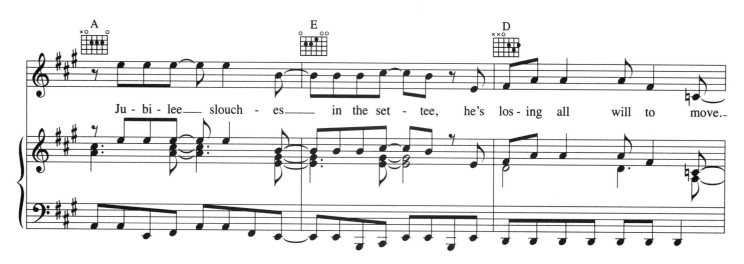

Ju - bi - lee___ slouch - es___ in the set - tee, he's los - ing all will to move..

He's gone div - vy, too much tel - ly,

he watch-ing twen-ty four ho-urs of rub-bish.   1. He's got bu - tane,
(Verse 2 see block lyric)

he's got plas - tic bags,— his eyes are go - ing square.—

He no ra - ver, just— an-ti-so - cial, he not go-ing to

cut his hair.— He dress-es in-cor-rect-ly, no-one told him,— se-ven-teen,—

no one told him, talk to girls.

(How to do it_____ but he's just too spotty.)

He dress-es in-cor-rect-ly, no one told him— se-ven-teen,— he not keen—

To Coda ⊕

— on be-ing like___ a-ny-one___ else. (So he just

plays on his computer game.)

Verse 2:
Jubilee's dad, Billy Banker
Thinks his son is a slob.
He should get out more, stop scabbing
He really should go and get a job.

15 THIS IS A LOW

Words & Music by Damon Albarn, Graham Coxon, Alex James & David Rowntree

⊕ *Coda*

Verse 2:
On the Tyne, Forth and Cromarty
There's a low in the High Forties
And Saturday's locked away on the pier,
Not fast enough dear.
And on the Malin Head,
Blackpool looks blue and red.
And the queen, she's gone round the bend,
Jumped off Land's End.

Verse 3: - Instrumental

16 LOT 105

Words & Music by Damon Albarn, Graham Coxon, Alex James & David Rowntree